SOULFUL UNCONDITIONAL GENUINE INSPIRATION

KRISHNA G

You meet someone, feel butterflies, and start pondering a future. You are pretty sure you are falling in love - or are you?

- Soulful Love

WHAT IS LOVE?

I thought I found true love
But the truth is true love found me
Love isn't a feeling that anyone can find
Love finds that someone on its own

I thought love is romance, hugs and kisses
But the truth is love is all about caring
Love isn't something you look for pleasure
Love builds with respect for each other

I thought love develops between four walls
But the truth is distance doesn't matter
Love isn't a thing that fails if not close
Love won't replace you if you are far away

I thought love is attraction among couples
But the truth is love is glimpse of heaven
Love isn't an object that you can buy
Love comes for free spontaneously

I thought love demands sacrifices
But the truth is love is growing together
Love isn't something for falling
Love is rising above together forever

AFFECTION

I try to make you happy with my own ways
Smile on your face brings smile on my face
It is a nice feeling to be in your thoughts
Gives me assurance that you love me lots

You reach out to me when i don't respond
It shows how much you respect our bond
I know deeply how much I mean to you
You hide the emotions all the way thru

You genuinely understand feelings of mine
No true expressions from you is just fine
I feel your affection through your words
Even if we live in two different worlds

You love to talk and listen to my voice
That genuinely makes my heart rejoice
I wish the time just stops then and there
My ears fill with stories that you share

You like my behaviour and companionship
That shows the depth of our relationship
You may have a genuine feeling for me
I surely won't mind to wait until eternity

THE WAY I SEE YOU

You look so beautiful and charming
Like a lovely sunrise in the morning
I try to appreciate your beauty
You just disregard with your modesty

Your pretty eyes just grant me peace
When you look, I get weak in my knees
I feel you always smile with your eyes
They always tell the truth, never ever lies

I am overly captivated by your lovely lips
They always say the most amazing things
Your sweet smile always fascinates me
It's so radiant, my face lifts up with glee

I notice your gorgeous luscious hair
The look that it brings in you is very rare
Love the forelock that falls on the face
Supplements your stunning beauty always

I always see you through my eyes
You are the most beautiful and wise
A lady with both beauty and brain
I always fall for you again and again

FEELING YOUR PRESENCE

Even when you are not here with me
I feel your presence wherever I see
You are miles away in deep sleep
I can feel your breath on my cheek

I imagine talking to you in my mind
It feels you are standing just behind
I can hear you whispering in my ear
The sweet voice I always wanted to hear

Your words are resonating in my head
Same lovely little things once you said
I can listen to your words all night long
So soothing as Prateek Kuhad's indie song

I feel your touch just thinking about you
You feel the same and that's my view
You are in my deep thoughts my love
I wish you were in my arms right now

SHE

You are beautiful the way you have always been
Not like the women that appear in glossy magazine
You are charming with a lovely little smile
Not like the ladies that maintain mediocre style

You are stunning like a full moon in the dark
Not like the ladies that don't appear to have a spark
You are elegant with a sparkle in your eyes
Not like the women that are not smart and wise

You are cute like a lovely little doll
Not like the ladies that are always sad and dull
You are gorgeous as a bright shining star
Not like the females that hide in a different avatar

AMOUR

It may not be obvious the way we pretend
I always knew you were more than a friend
We started off to build a great friendship
I think it's drifting to romantic relationship

I love to spend most of my time with you
Spread the romance all the way through
Your company has always been amazing
I am ecstatic how our relation is shaping

You are a bright star emitting all the light
I feel your soft warmth all day and night
You always recide deep in my heart
Even if the long distance keeps us apart

There is romance in the air when we speak
That's the moment my heart feels weak
My words may not be able to convince you
You know my feelings for you are so true

LOVE ONCE AGAIN

Lost my first love with immense pain
Never thought I will fall in love again
Felt my soul just died with explosions
Days just passed with painful emotions

When you crossed your path with mine
My heart whispered you are my sunshine
Fell for your lovely beautiful nature
Started feeling affection for a stranger

Your connection felt a breath of fresh air
Saw some hope, we can be a lovely pair
Sensed you brought back life in my soul
Winning you all over became my only goal

I thought my feeling for love disappeared
True love with your presence reappeared
Falling for you erased all my pain
It is a great feeling to fall in love again

HEART TO HEART

I like your words and your long talks
Can't wait long for you to come back
You are a magnet that I feel attracted to
Now I know why I am falling for you

I look at the window, your face appears
In a jiffy don't know where it disappears
For a while I feel you stood there
Now I know I imagine you everywhere

I walk on the street thinking about you
Just forget the purpose where I headed to
Love you being in my thoughts always
Now I know how I spend my beautiful days

I love your eyes, your smile & your honesty
You are an open book with some dignity
Love your attitude with no masks on face
Now I know why I crave for your embrace

I know what is so special about you
That's the reason I am totally in to you
Moments spent with you are priceless
Now I know why you are so precious

DREAM

It is close to midnight
You have arrived in my dreams
Let's count the stars together
Laying under the trees

I wish this beautiful night
Doesn't see the morning
You lay in my arms all night

And I just keep on dreaming

YOUR PIC

I know a picture speaks thousand words
A glimpse of you stops my heart of hearts
I look at you and jump in to dreamworld
Never wish to come back to the real world

When I see your pic my heart skips a beat
Your charming face sweeps me off my feet
Your bright eyes shine like stars above
Sweet smile of yours brings glee and love

No words to describe the way you look
Your love is enough to fill my empty book
I can write infinite words for you my love
Even then the count will not be enough

I got smitten by your beauty and grace
Your care for me is a comforting embrace
I try to let you know but unable to convey
Your depth of love brings me joy everyday

Your intelligence fills me with lot of light
I can't stop thinking about you day & night
I will love you always with all of my heart
You are the one for me right from the start

THOUGHTS

You are a sweetheart, so gentle and true
An amazing & lovely person, through and through
Your respect for my words is so rare and beautiful
I wish I had met you when my heart was not full

I met you when my love was a bygone memory
Now I find it hard to love again, it's not that easy
I am kindly obliged for the time you and I share
You are truly a gem of a person beyond compare

I wish you knocked, when my love was at the door
I could have fallen for you and loved you more
I wish somehow, I could just go back in time
And loved you with whole heart as if you are mine

I know you are one in a billion, a rare gem to find
A caring respectful gentleman, so loving and kind
The friendly approach of yours touches my soul
Your sheer presence in my life makes me whole

FRIENDSHIP VS LOVE

You give your whole heart to your love
They end up breaking your heart somehow
You give your broken heart to your friend
They end up providing all the help to mend

It is a fact that love comes and goes
The genuine friendship forever grows
Love brings joy, but also brings great pain
Friendship survives through sunshine and rain

Love is a flame that burns with desire
When it is tested it always turns in to fire
Friendship is a bond that is built on trust
If it breaks there is always room to adjust

Feeling of love fills the heart with glee
True friendship sets the feelings free
Love is a devotion that needs effort and care
Friendship is a gift that is available to share

YOUR ENTRY IN MY LIFE

You came into my life as a special surprise
Your positive attitude for me opened my eyes
The aura around you is made of a special blend
Now I can feel my love for you will never end

I cannot express the depth of my affection
You light up my world with your perfection
I cannot imagine what my life would be
If on that lucky day you hadn't met me

As the days passed, my feelings began to grow
I found myself falling deeper with a flow
My dearest sweetheart I just want to say
That I love you much more each passing day

You changed my life in the most amazing way
I want to thank you for this every single day
I'm so grateful for the love and affection we share
You have my promise that I will always be there

THINKING OF YOU

When sun's first light shines upon my face
My thoughts drift towards you at a quick pace
A thrill in my chest builds an enticement
My heart craves to talk to you in excitement

I feel those butterflies when I think of you
With an anticipation that I will speak to you
Now I can assure you , my love for you is true
Forever and always, my heart belongs to you

You are the one that makes my world bright
Together, forever our love will take its long flight
I know my one sided love for you runs very deep
If you wish, my heart is available for you to keep

The beat of my heart makes feel your presence
Every breath I take, I'm in a state of essence
When you are by my side, I feel a lovely breeze
My soul sings with joy and my mind feels at ease

LIFE WITH YOU

My love for you runs deep within my heart
Like the river and sea that can't be apart
There's never a moment that ever goes by
When I am not dreaming about you and I

The special moments that we are sharing
Happy memories for future we are shaping
You are my world, my love, my joy, my all
With you by my side, my heart feels tall

Our bond is strong, I know will never part
Together forever, you will be in my heart
I'll be there for you till the end of time
With your love, my love will always shine

When you smile, my world goes wild
My heart races and I act like a child
I can't imagine my life without you
With you my love, my skies are blue

LESSON LEARNED

Yesterday I was feeling so sick
Had No energy to go to the clinic
When I asked for help, oh dear
My old friend said no, I shed a tear

I thought our friendship was so true
Now I see that it's not, it's through
He says he loves me, but his actions speak
Contradiction in his words, my heart got weak

I thought love was pure and true
But now I see it's just to get laid too
My belief in love is shattered now
Endless tears I shed somehow

So now I know that people just use
When you need them, they bluntly refuse
I thought we had something much more
Now my broken heart is bitterly sore

Not trust everyone what I learned yesterday
And it's a lesson that I'll remember everyday
I never knew love is just a game to some
One day I will find true love and l will overcome

FAIRYTALE LOVE

We fell for each other just by chance
No doubt ours is a fairytale romance
Your light is there to guide me through
I promise, all the way I will follow you

Your love feeds my hungry soul
When I am low, it makes me whole
With wings of love you carry me
Our love is destined for eternity

We made a wish upon a falling star
That our romance will stay forever & ever
Our wishes will fly on wings of desire
Let them soar to the heavens and higher

Let's dream beneath the starry skies
And sip nectar of love from paradise
In your eyes I see us in this fairytale
Is this a dream or reality our love will tell

SOULMATE

Soulmate comes in life out of the blue
Not only in romance, but in friendship too
Special friend with whom we laugh and cry
Only person whom we trust under the sky

That special bond no words can express
A connection that relieves all the stress
A friend who understands you like no other
Who supports you like a sister or a brother

It may not be the romance that we seek
Their presence makes our soul feel complete
Only friend we call when our world's falling apart
Unhesitatingly they mend our broken heart

We know for us they will always be there
Good or bad times they always care
So don't underestimate the power of a friend
They may just be your soulmate in the end

THINKING ABOUT YOU

Whenever I think about fondness
I think about YOU
Whenever I dream in sleep
I dream about YOU
Whenever I feel warmth
I feel about YOU
Whenever I am happy
I imagine being with YOU
Whenever I believe in love
I just trust YOU
Whenever I anticipate respect
I admire YOU
Whenever I close my eyes
I only see YOU

MY FRIEND

I met a beautiful soul felt an amazing connection
We clicked right away she seemed the right person
We laughed, cried, had an amazing time together
We became very close and understood each other

She pulled herself away, rocky road was the reason
An emotional note I wrote, clarified my position
She came back to me, we laughed away at our rift
Life was normal again, our friendship got a new lift

Days, months passed, she tried to pull away again
I tried to mend differences, my efforts went in vain
She bid her final goodbye that left my heart in pain
Don't know in future we'll see each other again

I wish she was still with me as I deeply miss her
I know she has vanished from my life forever
I pulled myself together & dealt with the emotion
It is hard and painful, but I decided to move on

PAIN

My heart is heavy with the pain I feel
Betrayed by friends not easy to heal
In friendship trust is hard to come by
Finding a right friend is quite a try

When the friendship was built I was thrilled
Ignored me when their desires got fulfilled
No help was offered even when I was in need
Left my sore heart to bleed, bleed and bleed

My heart is broken, torn and shattered
Here there everywhere pieces are scattered
It's hard to pick them up to join and mend
Could be fixed with the help of a special friend

We search for love and we search for trust
Most of the times we end up in the dust
Feels good for a while until the truth is shown
Leaving us hurt, broken, depressed and alone

Such is life we must accept and move on
Hurt may linger until we find that special one
We'll bump in to a right & lovely person one day
And our broken hearts will finally mend that day

BEHELD AND SMITTEN

You have attractive eyes & your lips are so sweet
They light up my world & my heart skips a beat
Your smile just warms me all the way through
I didn't know what love meant until I met you

Dark circles under your eyes are a thing of beauty
They enhance your look to a gorgeous cutie
The glasses on your face I can't ignore
They invite me to love you even much more

With the words you speak my heart takes a flight
They just make me fall in love with speed of light
Your inner beauty shines it is very clear to see
That drew me towards you, now you belong to me

Your voice is so sweet, you talk like a song
I can listen to you non-stop all day long
Your speech inspires me and makes me happier
I am blessed and I promise I will love you forever

GIFT

She asked me what you want as a gift
With a smile I said you already gave it
Memories we had shared together
The best gift I have received ever

You have already given me so so much
Showered your love with a special touch
Memorable times I have spent with you
The moments seem like dream come true

Your presence in my life is so pleasant
Much more valuable than any present
You would be so kind I never knew
Just love me like that as you do

Remove the thought of giving a gift
Let's give our friendship a special lift
Let it bloom forever, bright and blue
Like the memories I have shared with you

YOUR LOVE

I see you when I close my eyes
You appear from far away skies
I'd like you to stay with me forever
As I open my eyes you disappear

I feel you when I open the window
The breeze of you gives me soft glow
I breathe you to keep myself alive
Without you I may not survive

In my heart forever you will stay
I'll be with you come what may
In your company I find paradise
I am always ready for any sacrifice

I see us together when I gaze at horizon
Happy and bright like a rising sun
Earth or heaven our love will persist
For timeless eternity it will exist

WISH

I wish I was a bird I could fly to places new
With wings to take me on a journey to you
Crossing mountains, valleys, rivers and oceans
To bask in your love and feel those emotions

I wish I was the wind I could softly caress
Your smooth silky hair and your pretty face
Flowing & moving all around my sweetheart
To feel the special warmth from your every part

I wish I was the moon I could spread soft light
Peeped through your window while you slept tight
When the night gets darker I would wake you
To always confess my special caring love for you

I wish I was the sun I could shine bright all day
With rays of love to warm your heart all the way
As you rise from sleep my love would display
A promise of joy making you feel loved everyday

I am just a voice I can only express thru words
Hope they find the way to your heart of hearts
Wherever you are and whatever you do
My love and care for you will always stay true

SORRY

I'm sorry for the hurt that I have caused
The way I reacted I could have paused
I genuinely never meant to make you cry
Unfortunately my words seemed to fly

I've been far away far too long
And my ways, they may seem wrong
Saying no is just a habit for me now
Didn't realise you will get hurt somehow

Your response caught me by surprise
Couldn't see tears in your eyes, I apologise
It was never my intention to be rude
My words just slipped that spoiled your mood

I couldn't sleep last night, my mind just raced
Thinking of you every minute as the time paced
Our bond is very strong and it will remain so
We'll grow even closer just want to let you know

I hope that you can forgive me my friend
Our relationship will continue without an end
My respect for you has grown a lot you know
Together our love will only continue to grow

TRAVEL/STAY

I don't want to take a gondola ride in Venice
I want to drown deep in your dreamy eyes
I don't want to climb Mount Everest
I want to lay beside you and take rest

I don't want to visit the Niagra falls
I want to hold you tight in my arms
I don't want a river seine cruise in Paris
I want to watch starry night in your eyes

I don't want to watch sunsets in Maldives
I want to venture your mind with deep dives
I don't want to see famous art in Hobart
I want to stay in your beautiful heart

I don't want to visit highlands of Inverness
I want to live in the sea of your tenderness
I don't want to walk on the streets of London
I want to go out with you for a lovely luncheon

I don't want to take any flight
I want to be with you and see the light
I don't want to travel the world
I want to be part of your lovely world

WISH FOR YOU

I wish I was rich enough to buy you an Island
But I promise I will never leave your hand
I wish I could reach the sky to pluck you a star
But I promise I will be with you wherever you are

I wish I could paint a lovely portrait of yours
But I promise I will paint you with my own words
I wish I could make a statue with water and dirt
But I promise I will treasure you deep in my heart

I wish I could write your name on all the stalls
But it's already written all over my heart's walls
I wish I could sing you my favourite love song
But my soul whispers your name all along

I wish I could swim across seven seas
But I have drowned in your sea of kindness
I wish I could travel across the world for you
But your world is mine and that is so true

IF I AM

If I am an artist you are my art
If I am a writer you are my story
If I am a poet you are my poetry
If I am a painter you are my painting
If I am a doctor you are my patient
If I am a musician you are my music
If I am a dancer you are my dance
If I am a player you are my game
If I am a photographer you are my photography
If I am an actor you are my acting
If I am a heart you are my heartbeat
If I am a lover you are my love

I can be anything, nothing will stop
you to be part of my world.

PLEASE DON'T STOP

You are the sweetest thing in my life
Without you I can't imagine my life
There is no one better than you
Please don't stop me loving you

You are a beautiful soul my love
Nothing could stop me falling in love
I can't think of anyone but you
Please don't stop me loving you

You are so kind, simple and warm
That made my heart feel so warm
There is something special in you
Please don't stop me loving you

You have occupied my heart
No one else but you in my heart
I just can't live without you
Please don't stop me loving you

PRECIOUS CONNECTION

When we meet someone our souls just glow
It is an amazing feeling very few of us know
It feels like we are part of the same chain
A divine connection that's not easy to explain

Sometimes in life, we meet a friend
Whose bond with us will never end
We want them to be with us, forevermore
Even if we never felt this feeling before

It is a match that is deeper than words
It is a feeling that soars like the birds
Two souls that were meant to align
And their friendship will always shine

A stranger with whom you connect so much
Keeping them close with a gentle touch
We must cherish the bond and hold it tight
It is a very rare and precious delight

FRIEND

I looked everywhere to find a good friend
Who would be with me until the very end
Someone whom I could keep close to my heart
With whom I would never drift apart

Then came that lucky day I bumped in to you
I sensed you are the one my instinct was so true
I think the almighty heard my silent prayer
Finding a friend like you it's truly very rare

SILENCE

From miles away in the sea the wave did grow
A nature's wonder that's a breath-taking show
As the massive wave crashed upon the shore
The calm & quiet shoreline felt its mighty roar

The feeling that the shore felt I feel you too
Even though there is silence between us two
Your presence always lingers in my mind
Like the wave that leaves the shoreline behind

I don't get to see you with my eyes
Nor feel your touch, nor hear your sighs
You must know I still sense you all around
As the shoreline senses the wave's sound

Not to worry about the silence my dear friend
I can deeply feel our bond will last until the end
The silence between us can't keep us apart
If both of us hold each other in our heart

YOU ARE SPECIAL

You are my best bright shining star
Who shows me the path in the darkest hour
Your loving heart is so pure and bright
You illuminate my path with your beaming light

Your beautiful smile fills me with ecstasy
My heart gets filled with happiness and glee
Your happiness is contagious and true
It brings me much closer and closer to you

When the rain falls and the winds blow
You hold me tight and never let me go
You walk with me through the stormy weather
Your love keeps me safe and warm forever

When I get emotional and tears start to flow
You are always there to wipe and let them go
You try to whisper caring words in my ear
And you remind me that you are always near

You are my umbrella in the rain
You are a torch that lights up my darkest pain
You are an angel who makes me feel free
You are the one who always stands by me

I WRITE BECAUSE YOU EXIST

I tap my fingers on phone and write
Words flow effortlessly that feel so right
My mind and heart stroll in the mist
I write because you exist

Words form sentences that are so true
I express my thoughts especially for you
Falling for you I couldn't resist
I write because you exist

The rhyming flows with each key stroke
The rhythm of my heart is not a joke
I convey my feelings without any twist
I write because you exist

Let the fingers tap and words rhyme
For every emotion exchanged over time
My love for writing will always persist
I write because you exist

YOUR SPECIAL ONE

I think you found that special one
Who loves you and only you my hun
Someone who appreciates your smile
And loves to be with you all the while

I think you met that special friend
Whose love for you will never end
Someone who appreciates your worth
And loves you to the end of the earth

I think you found that special someone
Who treats you as a special person
Someone who walks by your side
In his dreams with your stride

I think you met that special person
Whose care for you can be compared to none
Someone who cherishes all that you give
And will trust you as long as you live

DREAM GIRL

You are not just a friend you are my dream girl
My love for you is more precious than a pearl
I know you see me as a friend that I don't mind
Deep down your love for me is a different kind

You don't express your love but I can see
You hide your feelings for me secretly
I know you miss me when I am not in touch
Then you contact me I feel your love so much

My heart beats for you each and every day
I can't suppress my love whatever I try to say
You don't respond to my love which is okay
I will cherish my love for you come what may

I wish my sweet dreams become a reality
You keep loving me until the end of eternity
Express your love and let your feelings free
Together let's create a beautiful love story

YOU ARE MINE

My friend, our friendship isn't brand new
It reached a level where my heart beats for you
Our journey is like a dream come true
It is as beautiful as the sky when it is blue

Your soul is mine, my heart is yours
Love for you will last for many more years
You belong to me, I belong to you
Our sweet love will forever be true

You have got a million dollar smile
Your shining smile is truly worthwhile
Beneath your surface lies a mind that's wise
Connecting with you feels I won a grand prize

Hold me in your arms till the end of time
Whisper in my ear your sweet love rhyme
Take me for a walk on the road to heaven
Lay beside me forever in our romantic love den

SPACE

In a corner of my heart there is a little space
Only reserved for you, a holy sacred place
All my emotions are stored safe and secure
With all the love that's strong and pure

Your shower of love accumulates every day
The heart starts to expand in its own way
We may drift apart in a stormy weather
This space will ensure to bind us together

Deep within my heart this corner will be there
That will be filled with love, warmth and care
Time and tide can test our love whatsoever
Our love is true and will last forever

Be assured that you are secured in my heart
Your love is a precious piece that won't fall apart
Our bond and affection is real and true
This space will always be occupied by you

LOVE WITH ROMANCE

You wanted your world a wonderful sight
I entered your life to make your days bright
You trialled and took a chance on me
I opened my romantic heart for you to see

You took a deep dive in to my heart
I wanted you to tear my heart apart
You made my heart skip a beat
I wondered until now why we didn't meet

You decided to live in my heart forever
I thought and understood it's now or never
You painted your love in my heart
I preserved the painting that's a piece of art

You will be happy with me it's my vow
I will love you in all possible ways somehow
You being with me, life will be a dream
 I and you, we will make a perfect team

WORDS

Feelings flow in words for you my dear
I try to stitch those words together
They end up in a poem meant for you
That captures our beautiful love so true

Your heart is a friend of my heart
They talked to each other from the start
Love evolved as the time went by
Now they can't be separated even if we try

You bring the colours to my life I know
I mix my love and paint a rainbow
Your smile is a killer as it appears
Your laughter is music to my ears

Our hearts beat in a perfect harmony
Love between us is so pure and free
My words will express your beauty forever
I will write these poems for you year after year

BEFORE YOU

I was a blank book before I met you
With no letters on any page to view
You came in and spread your glory
And helped me write a brand new story

I was a wilted flower before I knew you
Few petals survived may be one or two
Your love watered me with a steady flow
The power of love made my petals grow

I was a lost ship before you met me
Without hope almost sunken in the sea
You found me and lifted my spirits
Made my heart happy beyond the limits

I was a deserted soul before we met
With a lot of pain I was very upset
In your kind heart I found my shelter
Gave my life a purposeful endeavour

LOVE HAS NO RULES

Love is an emotion it has no rules
It can make people emotional fools
It has the ability to make a heart sing
And can break the heart with bitter sting

Love has the strength to mend and heal
It can give a broken heart a happy feel
It has the power to break you again
And can make you suffer with intense pain

Love is a feeling that can set you free
It can also keep you in utter misery
It is a force that can't be controlled
And it won't stay long if you try to hold

Love can feel pretty wonderful
It can make one's life quite colourful
It is a gift that's worth receiving
And treasure it with amazing feeling

FEELINGS FOR YOU

Your hug was such a warm embrace
The warmth of your love I can't replace
My heart raced when you held me tight
The beautiful moment just felt so right

You looked at me with your alluring eyes
My heart jumped high to reach the skies
The stare of your eyes was a piercing gaze
I felt like a prisoner stuck in your cage

You held my hands for a little while
I felt a current that was worthwhile
The touch was a feel of gentle breeze
That passed through me with much ease

Your lips danced in rhythm when you spoke
The words were soothing like an old folk
The music of your voice was like a melody
That soothed my soul so sweetly

LOVE IS A MYSTERY

You fall in love with someone who doesn't care
Someone else falls for you that you aren't aware
You tend to ignore the love that you receive
But chase the person you know they will deceive

You get attracted to the ones who are fake
And realise so much later it was a big mistake
You don't respond to the person that loves you
But wait for the one you know their love isn't true

Your heart gets torn apart when they dump you
One that loves you always comes to your rescue
You never understand why they love you so much
And turn a blind eye to their true heavenly touch

You wonder why love always works this way
And why does it bring both joy and dismay
The heart doesn't understand and feels heavy
It is true when they say love is a mystery

MOVE ON

It hurts when someone causes you pain
Not worth at all falling for them again
They don't deserve your love my dear
Stay away from them and don't go near

They make you feel small and weak
And break you down when they speak
They try to control your every move
To satisfy their desires and inner groove

My dear you definitely deserve much more
Just try to forget them and simply ignore
You know how much you are worth
Settle for what you deserve on this earth

Stop pouring your energy down the drain
Anything you do to make it right will go in vain
Listen to my whisper in a gentle tone
Move on in life and leave them alone

THE GIFT OF FATE

You are a lover of my soul and my mind
I feel you inside me your heart is so kind
Your tender love flows through my veins
I fill it in my heart and assure it never drains

You can read the silence in my eyes
They dream about us flying to deep skies
You can see the sweet smile on my face
It lits up when I see your beautiful grace

You paint my happiness and all my joys
Your beautiful painting makes me rejoice
You sculpt my dreams once I go to sleep
Amazing dreams that I treasure to keep

You write lovely stories of my daily life now
I feel it is turning in to a book somehow
You have become my sweet soulmate
I consider you as greatest gift of my fate

CARE

You care for me so much that I can see
Good to know you also think about me
Glad that you always keep me in your mind
That's a great gratitude, you are so kind

It is true, love is not the only emotion
Caring for each other is also a devotion
I love the affection you show all over
My heart dances in your love shower

I promise you I will always be there
You will know how much I also care
You may not love me in a romantic way
But my love for you will never sway

I can't thank enough for your care
The bond that we formed is very rare
I care for you with my whole heart
You know I love you from the start

TRAVEL BACK IN TIME

If I got a chance to time travel to the past
I would have searched and found you at last
The path wouldn't matter who choses
Life with you would have been bed of roses

If life offered a choice once more to relive
I would live it all with you as long as I live
I wish our paths crossed much earlier
But it is always better late than never

If there was a hope to rewind my years
I would sail with you erasing all my fears
My heart would listen to all your love
We would get the blessings from up above

Love knows no time so happy for it to be late
It is a heavenly feeling to fall for my best mate
Together we will walk in this new-found pathway
And reach our final destination one special day

FREEDOM

I want to be free where my dreams take a flight
Flying all around the world forever in delight
I crave for freedom with my wings outspread
Travel like a free soul where my desires are led

I want to enjoy nature and dance in the air
Love to fulfil my dreams with heart full of flair
I wish to leave all my tensions & worries behind
And embrace my new journey with a fresh mind

I want to escape from the toxic locked cage
And make my presence felt at the world's stage
I wish to flatter my wings and travel afar
Enjoy beauty of freedom and shine like a star

The free life is what I have been dreaming for
And listen to the freedoms gentle whisper
I would love you to join me my special friend
Let's cherish our journey from beginning to end

Printed in Great Britain
by Amazon

24345200R00030